HOW TO FIND A
GOOD
CHURCH

Worth Calling Home

TODD M. SMITH

General Editor

WESTBOW
PRESS
A DIVISION OF THOMAS NELSON
& ZONDERVAN

WestBow Press books may be ordered through booksellers or by contacting:

WestBow Press
A Division of Thomas Nelson & Zondervan
1663 Liberty Drive
Bloomington, IN 47403
www.westbowpress.com
844-714-3454

ISBN: 978-1-6642-5406-0 (sc)
ISBN: 978-1-6642-5405-3 (e)

Library of Congress Control Number: 2021925661

Print information available on the last page.

WestBow Press rev. date: 01/10/2022

This book is dedicated to the family of Crossroads Community Church. The contents of this book come from what your leaders have learned watching you seek after the contents of this book for the past fifteen years.

All the proceeds from this book go to the TEN (Touch Eternity Now) Ministry which seeks to educate orphans and plant healthy churches. Visit www.toucheternitynow.com for more information.

CONTENTS

CHAPTER 1

The Process and Pitfalls of Church Shopping

Todd M. Smith

S o you're shopping for a new church. If you grew up going to church, picking one was super easy: you went wherever your parents went. Now you are the head of the search committee for a new church. Church shopping is tiresome and complicated; frankly, it is nothing like choosing your supermarket or dry cleaners. In fact, this is why we devoted Chapter Two to discussing when you need to leave a church.

Starting your search may be for a variety of reasons. Maybe you're in a new city or town and need to find a church. Perhaps you are a new believer in Jesus Christ and desire to find a good church home. Maybe your current church differs from your understanding of biblical principles or leadership is heading in a new direction that makes it impossible for you to stay. Solomon made it clear there are seasons in life. The pursuit of Jesus inside a local church is not always linear. So whatever season you find yourself in today, this question remains: what is your plan to find a good church?

Having a plan to find a good church is crucial because the church is crucial to God's redemptive plan through history. The local church is the hope of the world. The local church fulfills specific roles in God's plan of saving and sanctifying people. If you desire to be part of building the church of Christ (Matthew 16:18), you need to participate in a solid local church.

Your pursuit of a local church is much bigger than just you. Finding a church family is finding your place to join God in his mission to rescue the people of this planet. You will discover that when you find the right church, it becomes clear that the church needs you as much as you need it. The right church home will offer you the opportunity to partner with God not by sitting and soaking but through standing and serving. You are in a significant search that will have a direct, eternal impact on your life and the lives of countless others.

Before you look at the process, you should know this book is to help focus your attention on *what* you are looking for in a new church. To begin, here is a straightforward process to help frame your search for a new church home, thereby providing *how* to go about the search. These six steps are not exhaustive but they are essential.

1. Saturate. Saturate the process in prayer. Your deep longing for God will lead you to the right church. Make this a daily task while you are searching. Pray that he makes it abundantly clear which church to attend and what is the timing of your commitment to the new church body.

2. Seek. Seek a new church where you cannot only *get from* but also *give to* a church family. Most people look only for the *get* part and pay little attention to whether this is a place where they can *give* their lives away to others.

3. Search. Search the local churches. Remember: a church is where you will spend much time and where you will invite others in your community to join you. The keyword is *local*. Make it a habit to ask those in your community which church they attend. Listen for a church name that keeps coming up in conversations. And keep your eye out for Bible studies and groups at local coffee houses; ask them where they attend church.

4. Seek. Seek recommendations from various sources. Seminaries, associations, and denominations are usually good at recommending churches. If you have moved, then ask your previous church's leadership for recommendations. Don't just let Yelp do your church search for you.

5. Scour. Scour the potential church's website before you decide to visit. When you scour a website, look at every page available, from the welcome page to the sermons, leadership, statements of faith, outreach, events for youths and children, conferences, and recommended resources. You can learn so much about a church by looking at its website. The search for potential churches can be narrowed quickly.

6. Select. Select your "potential churches". Potential churches are the ones you will commit to visiting in person. Don't let livestreaming the worship service be your visit. You must physically see and experience the church body. The best way to set this up is to select three or four churches to visit and visit

each one three to four times. It takes three to four visits to the same church to know if this church could become a "target church". Target churches are the ones you will invest much time in visiting.

Remember: just one actual visit to a church can be misleading, either positively or negatively. Again, it is best to start with a small number; we recommend three to four. The visiting process could take six to eight weeks. Once the potential church visits are complete, you will hopefully have one or two serious target church options. At this point in the process, you pick one and start worshipping there until the Lord confirms this is the church or pushes you to try the next target church. Should target churches become depleted, then you begin the process all over. As you can see, a church search can take an entire year so be patient and purposeful in the process.

Now you have a framework for the search process. However, before you jump into what to look for in subsequent chapters, you should be aware of potential pitfalls to avoid.

Pitfall 1: Passive Search

Do not be passive about your church search. You need a church family soon. Be intentional about the process by being purposeful in the next step of the process. Too many people commit to a new church too quickly. Committing too soon can lead to hard choices ahead. Others start the process way too late.

Pitfall 2: Superficial Search

Commit to looking more deeply than the superficial things such as location, building, and your kids' choice. Remember: your kids don't pick their doctors or schools so don't let them be the ones who choose your church. Be committed to a deep-dive search.

Pitfall 3: Pessimistic Search

Stay positive and hopeful as it is easy to get discouraged. Important decisions take time. The best decisions take the most time. It will be easy to become impatient and settle. Commit upfront not to settle in this process. God is at work, and he uses crockpots, not microwaves.

CHAPTER 2

When Should You Leave Your Current Church?

Scot Overbey

If you follow the sport of international track and field, you are probably familiar with Jonathan Edwards's name. Edwards, a British triple jumper, is the current world record holder in that event and has been since 1995. That year, Edwards was undefeated in the triple jump, and while competing at the 1995 World Championships he became the first man to traverse sixty feet as he hopped, skipped, and jumped his way to a world record. Later, Edwards remarked that during the 1995 World Championships, "I felt like I could jump as far as I needed to." Not surprisingly, Edwards was named BBC Sports Personality of the Year.

Edwards won the silver medal in the 1996 Summer Olympics in Atlanta. Four years later, Edwards won gold in the 2000 Summer Olympics in Sydney. Edwards retired from the sport in 2003 as Great Britain's most decorated medal-winning athlete, having been a one-time Olympic champion, a two-time World champion, a European champion, and Commonwealth Games champion. Amazingly, Edwards's world record in the triple jump stands to this day—some twenty-six years later.

What's more fascinating about Edwards is that he was more famous for his Christian faith than his jumping ability early in his career. Much like Eric Liddell, the British gold medalist in the four-hundred-meter dash at the 1924 Summer Olympics in Paris, Edwards made it his practice not to compete on Sundays, which cost him a chance to compete in the 1991 World Championships. However, in 1993, after much deliberation and counsel with his father, an Anglican vicar, Edwards changed his mind, deciding that God had given him his athletic talent for him to compete on the world stage.

Despite this policy change, Edwards's faith remained strong. Edwards commented, "My relationship with Jesus and God is fundamental to everything I do. I have made a commitment and dedication in that relationship to serve God in every area of my life." During this time, Edwards served as the host of the popular BBC Christian television show *Songs of Praise*. At the height of his career, Edwards was making plans to attend Dallas Theological Seminary and study Israelology. However, in a stunning turn of events, in February 2007 it became headline news that Edwards had abandoned his Christian faith. "I just stopped believing in God," said Edwards. "I don't go to church anymore. Not at all." What happened? His Christian faith and the church had seemingly been so important to him his whole life, yet in 2007 he decided to leave it all behind.

The story of Jonathan Edwards is undoubtedly a tragic tale of a man walking away from his faith and leaving the church altogether. This story is instructive, however. As a believer, while you are probably not considering a departure from the Church as Edwards did, you may be thinking of leaving your local church.

The truth is people leave their churches all the time. Sometimes it is for a good reason and other times it is not. Pastors see their fair share of these exits and most exits are not for right reasons. It's true that not every local church is in good health. Some churches are toxic, others are gravely ill, some are dying, and some are dead. So when is leaving your local church justified? What are the right reasons to leave? When and why is it okay to leave your present church?

Here are seven reasons why it might be time to consider leaving your present church:

1. Absence of biblical preaching and teaching (Acts 2:42–46; Romans 10:14–15; 2 Timothy 3:14–20). The preaching has become moral TED talks.
2. Absence of the biblical ordinances of baptism and the Lord's Supper (Matthew 28:18–20; Matthew 26:26–28). There is no priority on these ordinances.
3. Absence of biblical accountability and church discipline (Matthew 18:15–20; 1 Corinthians 5:1–11). Personal sin is rampant and never addressed.
4. Absence of biblical mission (Matthew 28:18–20). The church has become inward focused.
5. Absence of biblical worship (Ephesians 5:19; Colossians 3:16). Worship has become a show and lyrics carry no meaning.

6. Absence of biblically-qualified leadership (1 Timothy 3; Titus 1). The leadership is not plurality of leaders.
7. Absence of prayer (Acts 2:42). Prayer is infrequent or absent from the service

These seven absences are helpful because they can help answer the question "Is the church being the church?" When it fails in those areas for an extended time, it may be time to leave.

It is important to remember there is no explicit teaching in the New Testament instructing believers when it is appropriate to leave their local church. Here is a great reminder: be slow to pick a church and even slower to leave a church.

Think about this: twenty-one of the twenty-seven New Testament books are letters written to churches (thirteen Pauline epistles, seven general epistles, and Hebrews). Revelation could be added to this list because it contains seven letters from the glorified Lord Jesus Christ to seven local churches. That's twenty-two of twenty-seven books or 81.5% of the New Testament. In each of these twenty-two books, the author, under the inspiration of the Holy Spirit, attempts to warn, admonish, instruct, encourage, and correct a particular local church and thus call them to a higher and healthier level of Christian experience and practice.

In other words, the overwhelming take away from the New Testament regarding local churches is that churches are messy and many, if not most, need some level of course correction. Based on this, you should always be slow to leave your local church.

It's important to remember the church is full of people and whenever you have people, you have conflict and problems. Before you hop, skip, and/or jump from your present church, if at all possible stay and try to be part of the solution. Sometimes, the greatest blessings in life are on the other side of difficulty. Maybe, just maybe, if you stick it out you will find it was well worth it.

CHAPTER 3

The Six Birthmarks of a Healthy Church

The Church began at Pentecost. Every year, it was on the Israelite calendar to give thanks for the first wheat harvest of the season. The New Testament celebration would be different. Thanksgiving would come, but something would arrive far greater than wheat to fill their barns. It would be the Spirit of God who would fill their hearts. Just like that, an Old Testament celebration turned into the birthday of the Church, birthed by the Spirit of God. The celebration consisted of people "from every nation under heaven" (Acts 2:5). An awe filled the streets of ancient Jerusalem. Peter, who was filled with fear and days earlier denied he even knew Jesus, now rose to courageously affirm Jesus as the answer to all the questions about the Old Testament Messiah. He told the story of the promise of a savior made by the prophet Joel that had now been fulfilled in the person of Jesus of Nazareth. Jesus had just days before been crucified by the mob wishes of the Jews. Jesus conquered death by his resurrection from the grave, and in his name forgiveness of sins was now possible. This was God's plan from the beginning.

With careful attention to the ancient words, Peter rebuked the Jewish people who had put Jesus to death and the people were "cut to the heart" (Acts 2:37). He taught them from the scriptures, connecting the dots of the Old Testament and bringing clarity to the story of the kingdom of God. Repentance over sin was the posture of every heart and baptisms were the overflowing acts of obedient surrender. Three thousand members strong, the church began.

It was a baby church, a healthy church. Not enough time had passed for it to become corrupted by men's ideas and human strategies to make it grow. The truth of Jesus was new and alive. People were living witnesses to the wonder of what the Spirit does in total transformation of human hearts. Doctor Luke captures a snapshot of the church as it was meant to be: a picture of vibrant joy and unspoiled spiritual health.

You need to have this picture of a healthy church from Acts 2 stapled to your brain. If you are to find a healthy church, you need to know what one looks like. What better way to know what one looks like than to uncover the health of that first local church in Jerusalem. In the following pages, you will discover the six birthmarks of a healthy church so you are able to navigate the often turbulent waters of church shopping. These signs capture what the Spirit was doing among those early Christians at that first local church. You may find your standard for finding a good church isn't what it ought to be. But you will now be equipped to rightly evaluate where to joyfully submit your life and family as committed members of a healthy local church. Acts 2:42–47 is the model of a healthy church.

> And they devoted themselves to the apostles' teaching and the fellowship, to the breaking of bread and the prayers. And awe came upon every soul, and many wonders and signs were being done through the apostles. And all who believed were together and had all things in common. And they were selling their possessions and belongings and distributing the possessions all, as any had need. And day by day, attending the temple together and breaking bread in their homes, they received their food with glad and generous hearts, praising God and having favor with all the people. And the Lord added to their number day by day those who were being saved.

Here are six birthmarks of a healthy church.

1. Biblical Preaching

Mark Spansel

And they continued steadfastly in the Apostles Doctrine.

—Acts 2:42

Preaching is the engine that drives the ministry of the local church. Error in the pews is a result of errors in the pulpit. Man-centered ministries are evidence of a man-centered pulpit. A God-exalting community of humble people who love one another is reflective of a healthy pulpit committed to preaching scripture authoritatively by a man who knows he is under God's authority.

The first birthmark of a healthy church is biblical preaching, where the word of God is held high and the glory of Jesus is prominent. The goal of preaching is not to make people moral but to let God's word bring a person into greater conformity with Jesus Christ's teaching. Look at Acts 2 again and consider just what Peter was doing as he preached the first sermon to the church.

Peter was not preaching a clever message based on his own ideas. He wasn't preaching a new message at all. Peter was recounting for his audience the promises previously made to the nation of Israel. He took his material from the Old Testament scriptures, first from the prophet Joel (Acts 2:17–21) and then from the pen of David (Psalm 16, Psalm 110). Peter took the very words of scripture, interpreted them for the people to understand within the historic context of which they were written, and applied those words to their current situation. Let's be as clear as possible: biblical preaching is preaching the Bible as God has revealed himself in the story of redemption. Preaching is not based on current events, the pet-subjects of the preacher, or the demands of the people. Biblical preaching makes the Bible clear for all who are listening.

We have established that preaching has content. The content is the story of God as recorded in the sacred scriptures. But let's push it a step further. Biblical preaching always has its sights on the work of Christ in redeeming lost sinners. This is the flaming hot center of all biblical preaching. Peter demonstrates this very thing as he reaches the climax of his Pentecost sermon. He rehearsed the promises of the prophets and poets of Israel, then with direct speech he declared, "Let all the house of Israel therefore know for certain that God has made him both Lord and Christ, this Jesus whom you crucified" (Acts 2:36). The story was always pointing to Jesus, and therefore biblical preaching must always point to Jesus.

As the story of God is unfolded and the work of salvation through Jesus is exalted, people are called to repent and believe. Biblical preaching is not a lecture intended to make people smarter. Biblical preaching is to make the dead live, turn sinners into saints, and turn enemies into friends. "And Peter said to them, 'Repent and be baptized every one of you in the name of Jesus Christ'" (Acts 2:38). The goal of biblical preaching is to create worshippers fully devoted to the glory of God in the face of Jesus Christ.

This first birthmark of a healthy church, biblical preaching, is exactly what the early church was committed to and precisely how every healthy local church today will be committed.

2. Qualified Leadership

R.W. Mackey

And they continued in the <u>apostles</u> doctrine and fellowship.

—Acts 2:42

Even a casual look at the Bible will reveal an essential basic truth to the reader: a group of people will soon reflect their leaders. Stated bluntly, as leadership goes, so goes the group. Perhaps this is why God placed such a high premium on leadership historically in Israel and expects it now in his church. Great detail is given in the Bible to ensure that leaders properly represent God and take his people in the direction he desires. Finding qualified church leadership is the most critical function in the search for a good church. Everything else in the church hinges on this.

Although the church has several layers of leadership (both male and female), this section will focus on the primary leaders, who are called pastors or elders in the New Testament. Here are four foundational qualifications of pastoral leadership.

Spiritually-Mature Men

In 1 Timothy 3:1–7 and Titus 1:5–9, the Apostle describes what God requires in the character of his church leaders. These qualities do not focus on secular success or clever dealings but upon a spiritually-mature man. Interestingly, the only measure of observable leadership is the man's home not his work. Since the church is described as a family in the New Testament, it's important to God that the man's proving ground for ministry is his family. In many ways, leaders in the church are more like fathers than any other relation. A respected father cares for his family in various ways just like an effective elder serves the church.

Question: Would I want this man to be a spiritual father in my life?

Proven Men

A strange-sounding command appears in 1 Timothy 5:22: "Do not be hasty in the laying on of hands." This passage tells the church to be careful and to take its time when selecting leaders. Suppose the choice for a leader is the choice for the church's future? Few wonder why this command appears. The wrong leader is far worse than no leader. In other words, the church should be fully aware of the qualifications for leadership and thoroughly check out a man's life before placing him in such an important position. Choosing leaders just because they are willing to fill an opening will result in a weak, ungodly, powerless church. The qualifications spelled out in 1 Timothy 3 and Titus 1 should be verified by God's people. Solid leaders will partner with God to build solid churches—no shortcuts and no exceptions.

Question: Is this church extremely intentional, patient, and careful in selecting leaders?

Pastoral Men

Jesus is known as the Great Shepherd and the Chief Shepherd in the New Testament, titles rich in meaning throughout scripture. Leaders in the church are commanded in 1 Peter 5:1-4 to "shepherd the flock of God." Shepherding involves knowing, feeding, mending, protecting, guiding, and generally serving God's people i.e., his sheep. Some leaders devote themselves full time to this and are paid by the church. Other leaders have jobs outside the church and shepherd as they are able. All work hard. All are vigilant. All are men of the Bible and of the Holy Spirit. These men are charged with leading the church and the church, in turn, is charged with following them as in Hebrews 13:17.

Question: Does this church have orthodox, caring, approachable leaders whose leadership is worthy of my allegiance?

Cooperative Men

Every reference in the New Testament to leadership within a local church uses plurals. The New Testament churches, which serve as the models for churches today, had more than one leader in each fellowship. Ideally, a church's leaders work in the company of other leaders. The New Testament knows nothing of a single, authoritarian leader in the church.

This plurality of godly leaders has some significant advantages: greater accountability, more people doing the work, broader representation of the people, more viewpoints in the decision process, and a variety of gifts present, to name a few. A godly leader is a man who is not proud and willful; he is willing to have his ideas challenged and to defer humbly to fellow leaders. Most importantly, this is the leadership structure given to the church by God.

Question: Does this church practice a New Testament leadership structure of a plurality of elders?

Of course, the Bible has much more to say about church leadership than the principles presented in this section. Our prayer, however, is that enough information is presented here to help you, our brother or sister in Christ, assume a whole-hearted relationship to a church that is doing his work in his way.

3. Holy Hunger

Ken Kistler

And <u>awe</u> came upon every soul.

—Acts 2:43

Lethargy.

Yuck! The word sounds boring.

Webster's dictionary defines lethargy as "the quality or state of being lazy, sluggish, or indifferent." Who wants to attend a church like that? Nothing about our savior Jesus Christ was lazy, sluggish, or indifferent, so it follows that his church, the representatives of Christ on earth, should never be lazy, sluggish, or indifferent either.

Why is lethargy in a church such an important issue? Consider what the church does. First, the church serves the great God of the universe by teaching his incredible story of sin, redemption, grace and glory. Second, the church speaks about humanity's broken existence and how its most profound need can be met only in the person and redeeming work of Jesus Christ, the Son of God. Third, the church sends out the people of God to proclaim the truth of God to a lost and dying world doomed to spend eternity in hell, as evidenced in the Acts of the Apostles.

Not one iota of the church's tenets (the proclamation of the message, the truth the church believes, or the goal the church desires to accomplish) should exude laziness, sluggishness, or indifference. Christ gave his life for the church; how can the church be lazy in serving him? The Holy Spirit of the living God dwells within believers in the church; how can they be sluggish in following him? The creator God bought his chosen people with the blood of his son and called them to reflect his glory to souls bound for the eternal fires of hell. How can the church ever be indifferent to their fate?

Lethargy in the church? May it never be.

Instead, a holy hunger should drive God's church to respond to that

21

gift. Laziness must be turned to action, sluggishness to strength, and indifference to passionate care for the glory of God and the salvation of men. The believers in Acts moved, worked, and served with a Spirit-driven strength. They pursued people for God. They met needs in their midst. They refused to revel in past success but instead pushed forward for the sake of the gospel.

The passion seen in holy hunger is a pursuit of personal holiness. The people are excited and expect to be conformed to the image of Christ. They long for sanctification and actively practice repentance.

Find a church that has a holy hunger for God and his great commission. Ask church members what God is doing in their midst. Listen for passion from the pulpit. Don't bother to count the number of programs but look for love for people. Is there a reverence and awe of God? Is there faith in the strength and sufficiency of his word? Is there a recognition of his movement and work? Are there only nice platitudes or does biblical action follow biblical truth? Is there any evidence of the Spirit of God moving in their midst?

The New Testament church in Acts was a church of awe and action, not sluggishness or indifference. God's working in their midst excited them to more good works. That's the type of church our communities need and that's the type of church worthy of pursuit.

4. Uncommon Unity

Kim Miles

And all who believed were together and had all things in common.

—Acts 2:44

Unity among believers is mentioned in the New Testament so often you can't miss how important it must be. It's the first thing Luke says as he writes about the earliest Christians in Acts 2:44-45. Paul frequently talks about unity in his letters to the churches he had planted. You see his plea for unity in Philippians 2:2: "complete my joy by being of the same mind, having the same love, being in full accord and of one mind." Peter gives similar instruction in 1 Peter 3:8: "Finally, all of you, have unity of mind, sympathy, brotherly love, a tender heart, and a humble mind." As Jesus prayed for those who would come to believe (meaning us) in John 17, he prayed for our unity "that they all may be one."

How is uncommon unity displayed in a healthy local church? We suggest three things to look for:

A Joyful and Caring Community

Based on what you read in Acts 2, the early Christians apparently lived in wonderful harmony worshipping God, sharing meals, and enjoying body life together. Further, they shared their resources and made sure that everyone's needs were met.

- Do you sense a body that enjoys being together?
- Do you see and feel a real joy in the church's worship?
- How does the church care for the body and meet needs, both informally and through ministries?

Diversity of Gifts with Unity of Purpose

You might not intuitively link the concepts of diversity and unity but that's what Paul does as he discusses spiritual gifting in 1 Corinthians 12 and Ephesians 4. In a healthy church, members joyfully use their diverse and unique gifts to serve where God has planned regardless of their role—large or small, up front or behind the scenes—resulting in a unified, fully functioning, and healthy body.

- Do you see people joyfully serving and using their gifts?
- Are there opportunities in the church to serve and are worshippers encouraged to do so?

One Mind

In Philippians 2:2, Paul talks about a church "being of the same mind" and "being in full accord (unified) and of one mind." Is he perhaps emphasizing the importance of being unified? In a healthy church, the leadership (staff and elders) and the congregation should speak and act as a united community, on the same page with doctrine, purpose, and culture.

- Ask members of the body and leadership basic questions about the church; do you hear some consistency?
- How does your church view the Bible?
- What would you say is the purpose or mission of the church?
- How often do you hear the gospel expressed from the pulpit?
- Do you sense that congregants and leadership are tracking together?
- If the church publishes a doctrinal statement, is it consistent with feedback from leadership and congregants?

5. Joyous Worship

Greg Clark

They ate their food with gladness and simplicity of heart,
praising God and having favor with all the people.

—Acts 2:46–47

The believers in the early church gathered to praise God joyfully. This act of worship flowed from hearts that were Spirit-filled, proclaiming the greatness of the Savior and worshipping him for his continual provision. As musical worship is considered, you must look to this early gathering of believers to guide what congregational worship should look like. The early church's offering of worship mirrored the description Jesus gave of what true worship should resemble. He said, "But the hour is coming, and is now here, when the true worshippers will worship the Father in spirit and truth, for the Father is seeking such people to worship him. God is spirit, and those who worship him must worship in spirit and truth" (John 4:23–24).

When we worship God in spirit, we engage our whole being, including our emotions. This engagement is how God desires to be worshipped. Just as a young child jumps with joy when he or she reunites with a loving parent, so the worshipper is filled with joyful gratitude when beholding the wonders and splendor of God the Father. Jesus said that true worshipers will worship in spirit because full engagement is the natural response to God's glory. This is what Spirit-filled worship looks like.

- The congregation is physically engaged in the singing.
- There is a healthy excitement and joy among the congregation.
- Voices are lifted loudly and without shame.
- Worship leaders are humble and authentic.
- Congregants view themselves as the choir.

Spirit-led engagement must be informed by biblical truth. Worshipping God in truth is to worship the God of the Bible alone. Therefore, the lyrics a worshipper sings must describe, with precise biblical accuracy, the God of the Bible's true nature, characteristics, and deeds. This is called truth-filled worship.

This is what truth-filled worship looks like.

- All lyrics are rooted in scripture.
- Lyrics have doctrinal depth and are not just feel good word candy.
- The worship leader equips the congregation to understand biblical truths within a song.
- Scripture is used within the time of musical worship.
- Prayer is practiced within the team of musical worship.

Some basic questions to ask yourself as you visit a worship service:

- Is what I'm singing biblical truth?
- Is the congregation engaged?
- Is there a sense of humility from the musical leadership?
- Is God the focus of the musical worship?
- Is the aim of the service praise or production?

6. Impactful Evangelism

Jim Stitzinger

And the Lord added to the church daily those who were being saved.

—Acts 2:47

Telling others about Jesus is the joy of a church. We have the only message that transforms lives and the privilege of delivering it to everyone we know. A church that experiences impactful evangelism will "Go into all the world and preach the gospel to all creation" (Mark 16:15). The signs of impactful evangelism of a church are identified by the following.

Being Quick with the Gospel

People in the church know the gospel message backward and forward. You hear key verses that capture the heart of the good news of Jesus in 2 Corinthians 5:21, John 3:16, and Romans 10:9 to name a few. They explain God's holiness, our sinfulness, Christ's death and resurrection, and our need for repentance.

Congregational Integrity

The apostle Peter wrote, "Keep your behavior excellent among the Gentiles" (1 Peter 2:12). God's glory and a church's testimony depends on holy living. What do people say in the community when you mention the church's name? A clear and accurate gospel is portrayed by leaders and congregants.

Prayer for the Lost

The hard work of evangelism begins on your knees in prayer. The church knows God goes before them to work in the hearts of those people. They recruit others to pray for their unbelieving friends. They regularly pray for the lost from the pulpit.

Creating of New Mission Fields

The church is always looking for new ways to interact with unbelievers. For example, they meet in neighborhoods, join community events, volunteer at a hospital, have dinners at a rescue mission, join in a city sports team, and so on. Their goal is to consistently be "salt and light" (Matthew 5:13–16).

The apostle Paul told the Corinthians he delivered to them "as of first importance what we also received, that Christ died for our sins according to the Scriptures" (1 Corinthians 15:3). A church with maximum gospel impact will make delivering this message to unbelievers a matter of first importance!

Final Thoughts

The signs of a healthy church are not a mystery. They were both demonstrated and taught by the apostles in the first local church. It's also the case that these signs of health are not to be worn as a badge of superiority. Those churches where these six birthmarks are understood and practiced are also the least likely to make much of what they do right. They don't want to make much of what they are doing because they are too busy seeking to make much of Jesus.

These signs of health hang together on the head of the church,

King Jesus. They are not isolated programs of the church, but all of them point us to the one who died for the church. Biblical preaching points people to the finished work of Jesus. Qualified leadership calls people to follow Jesus. A holy hunger captures our attention with the beauty of Jesus. Uncommon unity reminds us we are all recipients of the manifold grace of Jesus. Joyous worship proclaims our devotion to Jesus. And impactful evangelism sends us out to celebrate Jesus for the watching world to see.

These birthmarks are not the invention of man and no man is the hero of the church. Jesus alone is worthy of our worship and the center of all a healthy local church does. So, friend, when you forget which sign is which and you're desperately trying to recall the proper way to diagnose church health, ask "Is Jesus at the center of all they do?" And you'll be just fine.

CHAPTER 4

What are the Secret Ways You Can Learn about a Church?

Jim Stitzinger

Church advertisements often make similar claims about their culture and ministry. They use familiar buzz words to emphasize dynamic worship, in-depth teaching, personal small groups, and an engaging children's ministry. Yet, how can we know if a church practices the claims they make? Thankfully there are many ways to discover its theology and methodology while separating current actions from aspirational goals.

As previously noted in Chapter One, the best way to explore any church is to visit over a period of time. Asking questions, experiencing the ministry, and learning the culture is always best done in person. Yet along with that exposure, here are twelve ideas to help you figure out the true health of a church:

1. Doctrinal Statement: Some churches take a minimalistic approach, publishing only a summary of their theological positions. Others provide a much more in-depth explanation of their positions. Look for clarity on the gospel, authority of scripture, and lordship of Christ. Do your research to find out if their statement and position papers are copied from another church or denomination

2. Sermon Archives: Listen to a cross-section of sermons listening for how the pastor communicates with the congregation. Is the preacher moving systematically through books of the Bible? Does the preacher teach thematically or topically as needed on particular issues that arise? How evangelistic are the sermons? Does the preacher expect that people are looking at their own Bibles?

3. Biographies: Where have the pastoral staff been trained? Their training will be a strong indicator of the theological and methodological trajectory of the church. Are all the staff from one institution or is there a variety of training influences? Additionally, what can you learn about the elders? How does their training and experience shape the way they shepherd the church?

4. Denominations and Associations: What formal or informal associations is the church connected to? Do they have denominational alignment (for example, SBC, C&MA, EFCA), administrative associations such as the Evangelical Council for Abuse Prevention (ECAP) or the Evangelical Council for Financial Accountability (ECFA), or support networks (9Marks, City to City, Acts29, SEND Network)?

5. Community Impact: How do people in the area perceive the church name? Does the city utilize the church's resources when community events, such as notable funerals, tragedies, prayer meetings, or blood drives, occur? Unbelievers will typically be very honest and direct regarding how a church is known. Is the fruit of the Spirit lived out by the church and easily identified by even casually-aware people?

6. Heroes and Friends: Who fills the pulpit in a guest capacity as a preacher or conference speaker? Those invited to serve in that role will bring a particular influence, culture, or teaching philosophy. Their presence is often indicative of what the church affirms and the direction they are heading. The same is true for recommended resources and books promoted.

7. Diversity of Gifts: Are spiritual gifts on display in a wide range of ministries, or is it more of a single-dimension ministry where one expression of gifting supersedes others? Is it a place where church leadership guides believers to serve according to their gifts or are congregants burdened by the heavy hand of administrative permissions? Do ministries arise from the congregation or do they always arise from the top down? Does the church leadership make it easy for members to use their time and talents to serve the body and community?

8. Team Tenure: A high turnover isn't always negative as some churches are sending churches, training leaders and mobilizing them to serve elsewhere. But high turnover can also be indicative of an unhealthy staff culture. Is the pastoral staff energized and supportive of each other's gifts and abilities?

9. Discipleship Pathway: Is there a clear pathway for spiritual growth through formal discipleship, equipping classes, mentoring opportunities, and biblical counseling?. What curriculum and books guide the studies? In an informal way, is there a pattern of Titus 2 older men and women investing in younger believers? Is the pastoral staff actively involved in dynamically shepherding the church?

10. Outreach: What evangelistic impact is the church having on its community? If the church ceases to exist, would the community know it was gone? Does it have homegrown missionaries deployed in Christian service? Is there a plan and pattern of church multiplication? Even a short time spent with a church should leave you with the distinct impression that it is deeply involved with local and international gospel proclamation.

11. Membership Covenant: In glancing through the membership materials, you will quickly see what it means to be part of the church family. Do they unite around core doctrines and holy living? Or do matters of preference creep into the covenant too? Are they identified by what they stand for or against? Does it include an agreement of confronting sin and restoring one another?

12. Kingdom Culture: A church filled with love for Christ, awareness of the Spirit's presence, and bold proclamation of God's word will be a place flowing with joy. Is this a joyful body of believers? Is this a church family that celebrates salvation and highlights the step of obedience in a believer's baptism? Is communion a time of special focus as Christ intended? Are the "one-another's" easily recognized as evidence of God's grace?

We call these secret ways to discover a church because they are often overlooked when checking out a new church. Do not get caught up in the refined marketing pieces and sophisticated campus layout. The church's health will always flow from its commitment to the authority of scripture and exaltation of Jesus Christ. The answers you find to these points will help you discern if this is the right environment for your spiritual growth.

CHAPTER 5

*You Found Your Church
Home. Now what?*

Ed Boness

But I, brothers, could not address you as spiritual people, but as people of the flesh, as infants in Christ. I fed you with milk, not solid food, for you were not ready for it. And even now you are not yet ready, for you are still of the flesh. For while there is jealousy and strife among you, are you not of the flesh and behaving only in a human way? For when one says, "I follow Paul," and another, "I follow Apollos," are you not being merely human? What then is Apollos? What is Paul? Servants through whom you believed, as the Lord assigned to each. I planted, Apollos watered, but God gave the growth. So neither he who plants nor he who waters is anything, but only God who gives the growth. He who plants and he who waters are one, and each will receive his wages according to his labor. For we are God's fellow workers. You are God's field, God's building.

—1 Corinthians 3:1–9

Do you remember when you were in elementary school and the teacher tasked you with creating a work of art to give to your parents? Can you remember hearing the vision behind what you would create, design, and deliver to your mom or dad? Can you remember working your hardest on that Mother's Day card and the joy she had when she picked up your glitter bombed, gluey, sticker-infested, misspelled work of art? Without a doubt, she was thrilled and that piece of artwork probably spent the better part of a year on the fridge.

Now fast forward to the last time you sent a note, birthday card, or gift to that same parent. What did it look like? Once misspelled words have been made right and a sense of maturity is evident in your writing and creativity. If you delivered the same level of work as an adult you once produced as a child, your parent might be concerned about your development. Similar maturity misdevelopments can happen in the life of a believer, and they seem to always be evident in the involvement in the local church.

In 1 Corinthians 3:1–9, Paul addresses the spiritual babies of the church at Corinth. They have grown old not grown up in the faith. Those spiritual babies are similar to the adult delivering a childish, Mother's Day glue-and-glitter card. Paul makes it clear: they are better and more mature than they have been acting. This passage will help answer the questions of what to do now you have found a new church home and how to avoid the pitfalls of the Christians at Corinth.

Paul first makes an effort in verses one and two to tell the churchgoers at Corinth that maturity is expected. He notes the inability of the believers in this church to even comprehend the letter he writes. Paul makes these supposedly mature Christians aware they need to grow up. Much insight is gained from a passage like this. You avoid a lot of potential hurt when you realize the first level of understanding, although essential and evangelistic, revolves around the basics of Christianity. The passage stops short of where true maturity in Christ should take you. You go from being the evangelized to being the evangelist, from student to teacher, and from baby to adult. All aspects of life revolve around a basic understanding that things that are alive will grow. The believer is no exception. Regardless of what Bible-teaching, Christ-honoring church you end up at, it's expected you mature.

Second, Paul notes in verses three and four that this church is not only immature but also grossly divided. He tells them that unity will bind them. After calling them fleshly, non-spiritual people, Paul notes jealousy and strife in their religious associations. Whether a Paul follower or an Apollos follower, Paul says enough is enough; the pastoral fan clubs have divided the church. This passage has vast implications for your new church home.

This party attachment to a pastor is a big part of our modern, constantly streaming, on-demand American Christian culture. You can go online and hear sermons from pastors worldwide and then dive deep into their archives. Although primarily a blessing, this can quickly turn into a curse. You can become so rich in resources you forget you have only become a family member of one church. You tithe resources to this church. You serve and give time to this church. You sit under the teaching of this pastoral team under Christ and the leadership of one elder board of shepherds under the Chief Shepherd Christ. As someone who floats in online for the occasional sermon here and there, you are not much more than a mere fan of that pastor or preacher.

Although a rich resource to enjoy, you must see this passage for what it is: a warning to the mere fans. Unity hangs in the balance when a church body becomes more consumed with the teaching they hear outside their church walls than the teaching coming from within. Focus primarily on maturing in Christ right where you are and keep yourself determined to use secondary preaching resources as just that—secondary.

Next, Paul shares in verses five to eight that humility should mark you. Paul continues his analysis of the Corinthian state of mind and follows this flawed thinking to its absurdity. "What then is Apollos? What is Paul? Servants," he says, "just merely servants that God has assigned to you."

The Apostle Paul refers to the vineyard worker as an illustration, where he makes it evident that those who labor in the field are hired hands. They offer nothing pertaining to the God-sized, supernatural work needed for actual growth and fruit bearing to occur. Paul states the planter and waterer are just laborers, and God uses them.

Similarly, the Christ-follower in the local church should see Paul's example of humility and follow suit. Paul had reason to boast but didn't. Christ's humble example is what Paul modeled. Your calling is the same. Humility should be evident in your character. Your life should be lived in the awesome wonder of the grace that God shows you through the Lord Jesus Christ, and your involvement in the church should be no exception. It is a gift to your new church when you enter with a posture of availability, humility, and teachability. A great testimony being evident in your life is that you are a contributor to the church not a critic. Engage and actively support your leaders.

Finally, Paul notes in verse nine that ministry is waiting for you. Notice that Paul assumes labor at the end of verse eight almost as a challenge, saying that "each will receive his wages according to his labor." Paul notes that the Corinthian church is the field where work is happening. Who owns the field or church in which you are serving?

God does. Everyone inside of the church is, as Paul puts it a few verses earlier, a worker. Paul is a worker, and Apollos is a worker, each of the Corinthians in the church at Corinth is a worker. So what about you? Are you a worker in your new church home?

It's funny how obvious the flow of this passage becomes. When you grow up and mature in Christ, you will naturally desire to guard unity in Christ. Your humble response to protect that unity will lead you to wise up and ultimately lead you to get up and get involved in working for Christ. Engaging in a ministry opportunity in your new church is the clear end of this chapter. Maybe you have located your new church home and you need to pursue membership, or perhaps you are now a member and looking for the next step; the answer is to start serving. Where, you might ask. The answer is anywhere. Just start somewhere.

In 1 Corinthians 12:12–27, Paul makes much of the ordinary believer who has a gift the church is waiting to enjoy. There is beauty in diversity and sweetness in good harmony. Churches need their members fully engaged in their church not robbing the congregation of their gifts. Every part of you should be fully involved in your new church. Your children, your weekly attendance, your giftedness, your primary instruction, your discipleship in small groups, your practical guidance through friends and pastors, your resources through time, talents, and treasure are examples of what being fully involved means. It's time to get fully engaged and bring all of who you are into this new body.

Think back to the work of art analogy at the start of this chapter. Are you an illustration of a sad, floundering, misdeveloped, concerning case of yet another immature Christ-follower? Be different and stand apart. Do what living things do and grow up. Plant roots in your new church and bring everything about who you are there.

Your maturity, unity, humility, and ministry, are needed there. Your new church needs you.

CHAPTER 6

Your New Church Home Needs this from You

Todd M. Smith

The church of Jesus Christ is not an organization; instead, it is an organism. In the business world, a company is an organization and the organization has competitors. Competitors keep businesses on their toes because they know their competitors would love to see them stumble. The local church does not have a competitor. It has an enemy, a roaring lion seeking to devour the organism whole. This reality is why your new church needs something concrete from you.

Before defining the one thing, let's be clear that your church does not need you to be a consumer, camper, critic, or creaster. A consumer is just at church to take and bake: take from the church what you want to bake at home. Your church does not need a camper. A camper parks and sits around a campfire then packs up and leaves. If you are merely warming a seat, your church needs you to move on; they need that seat for the athlete who will take the field and participate. Your church does not need a critic. Critics never create anything. Criticism is not a spiritual gift. And nobody is more critical of themselves and the ministry than the leadership. Find out what your church is doing right and praise them for their faithful ministry. Learn to be a gift, not a grievance. Finally, your church does not need another creaster, a person who only attends on Christmas and Easter. If you only attend a church for those holidays, you are not looking for a church; you are looking for a holiday activity.

Every local church has real and pressing need of time, talents, and treasures. You will never see a No Help Wanted sign in the lobby of any healthy church. Churches operate on the currency of faith, trusting that God will supply all their needs. And God does just that for his church. God does this through his people by gifting them with time, talent, and treasure. Yet, there is a more intangible essential that your church needs, your pastor needs, and the church's leadership needs. Remember what was shared in the opening of this book: "your new church needs you more than you need it." If it is not time, talent, and treasure, what is this one gigantic need of your new church? The simple answer is supportive engagement.

If supportive engagement is so crucial to your church, then what exactly is it? Supportive engagement is when a follower of Christ joyfully and willingly submits his or her life to the ministry and leadership of the church (Hebrews 13:17). This person becomes an active part of the church family and immerses himself or herself inside the body. This person carries himself or herself with authentic joy and active support of the mission and ministry of the church.

When you make yourself invaluable to your church and do this by serving other people with joy, you naturally become supportively engaged. Do you remember Dorcas, the woman Peter raised from the dead, described as being "full of good works and acts of charity?" In Acts 9:29 Luke writes, "When Peter arrived, they took him to the upper room. All the widows stood beside him weeping and showing tunics and other garments that Dorcas made while she was with them." Dorcas was a supportive engager. She loved people so much and did so much good that the whole community mourned when she died.

Most churches have people who make the weekend worship service, the public gatherings of the church, a low priority. These are the people who only come to church when convenient and who use any excuse to miss a day or miss a service. A supportive engager sees a weekend worship gathering as an utmost priority (Hebrews 10:25). Supportive engagers see the week as just preparation for corporate worship and corporate worship as preparation for the week. As they look ahead, they do first things on the first day of the week, first by engaging in corporate worship. Today is the day to begin elevating the importance of church community in your life.

Since you have learned what your new church needs from you, the time has come to either start or finish the process of supportive engagement. The local church is the hope of the world and your new church is the hope of your community. You are about to find your place in his kingdom, and when you do, it will be your opportunity to kick a dent in eternity.